THE WORLD Beard AND Moustache CHAMPIONSHIPS

THE WORLD Beard AND Moustache CHAMPIONSHIPS

The First Official Book

Written by Michael Ames
with F Stone Roberts

Photographed by
Link Roberts
Brendan Burke
Larry Letters
Kyle C. Parsons
Tobias Nilsson

Published by Bloomsbury Publishing, New York and London
Distributed to the trade by Holtzbrinck Publishers

First published in the UK in 2004 by Boxtree,
an imprint of Pan Macmillan Ltd

Library of Congress Cataloging-in-Publication Data has been
applied for.

ISBN 1-58234-568-6

First U.S. Edition 2005

10 9 8 7 6 5 4 3 2 1

Printed in Great Britain by Bath Press

2003 WBMC Event produced by Phil Olsen

Stick your photo here

Above: Hot favourite
for the next World
Beard and Moustache
Championships
in Berlin, in 2005

Contents

Introduction

"The most important thing in life is style. That is, the style of one's existence – the characteristic mode of one's actions – is basically, ultimately what matters."

Tom Robbins

Since the first World Beard and Moustache Championships were held in Hoefen/Enz, Germany in 1990, the WBMC has grown beyond its humble regional origins. From a sporting collection of mostly German beard clubs in the early 1990s, the WBMC has become a truly global event. Since those early competitions, championships have since been staged in Norway, Sweden and in 2003, the United States.

The men of the 2003 World Beard and Moustache Championships come from everywhere. They do everything. There is nothing political, national, religious or occupational tying together this international cast of bearded characters.

What does unite them, what brought them to compete in Carson City, Nevada, is a simple and universal quality: individuality. Pure, unencumbered, and vibrant, these unique individuals and their extraordinary faces compel you to hold this book and look on curiously, bemused. They are stylish creations worthy of lingering study.

Some may find them unattractive. *Eccentric. Bizarre. Weird.*

The barbate men who fill these pages are not ordinary. They do not pass through your world unnoticed.

No, these mustachioed, goateed and bearded individuals are strutting peacocks of male facial fashion and their vanity is deserved. They work hard for their Handlebars, their Fu manchus and Imperials. Every morning, Elmar Weisser of Schoemberg, Germany spends 1 hour 45 minutes – with his wife's attentive aid – preparing his intricate Freestyle Beard.

The plumage is not, however, limited to faces. From the aristocratic strut to a swaggering braggadocio, a full range of eccentric styles is on display at the 2003 WBMC. The style each competitor chooses will define him in the months and years leading up to the Championships. As official WBMC Judge and Carson City Mayor Ray Masayko said, "The whole package will be judged; each element must complement the other."

There are 17 distinct categories from which one Overall Title will be awarded. The Best in Show will be a triumph, a coup of great proportion. The audience clamours for a better view. The judges eye one another and sweat. Flash bulbs ignite. One winner will emerge.

CATEGORY I

Natural MOUSTACHE

CATEGORY I

Natural Moustache

Facial areas more than 1.5 cm (0.6 in) past the corners of the mouth will be shaven. No artificial styling aids permitted.

1999, 2001 Defending World Champion: Vlado Livaja – Hoefener Bartclub; Germany.

2003 World Champion:
Cosimo Lepore – Italy.

2nd: Arne G. Jacobsen – Den Norske Mustachclub; Trondheim, Norway.
3rd: Bram Rosenfeld – Hong Kong.

The 2003 World Beard and Moustache Championships drew 123 competing delegates from 12 American states and 11 countries.

Previous spread: Cosimo Lepore – Italy
Opposite: Dan Sederowski

CATEGORY 2
English MOUSTACHE

CATEGORY 2

English Moustache

Narrow moustache; very long whiskers begin at the middle of the upper lip, are pulled to the side and slightly curled; both ends point slightly upward; areas past the corners of the mouth will be shaven. Artificial styling aids permitted.

1999 World Champion: Lutz Giese – Berliner Bartclub; Berlin, Germany.
2001 Defending World Champion:
Arno Dierkes – Kurpfaelzischer Bartclub; Heddesheim, Germany.

2003 World Champion:
Tony Papai – Germany.

2nd: Ferdinand Romankiewicz – Belle Moustache; Leinfelden-Echterdingen, Germany.
3rd: Lutz Giese – Berliner Bartclub; Berlin, Germany.

Opposite: 1999 World Champion Lutz Giese – Berliner Bartclub; Berlin, Germany

CATEGORY 3

Dali MOUSTACHE

CATEGORY 3

Dali Moustache

Narrow moustache; long points bent or curve steeply upward; areas past the corners of the mouth will be shaven. Artificial styling aids permitted.

2001 Defending World Champion: Joachim Schlender – Kurpfaelzischer Bartclub; Heddesheim, Germany.

2003 World Champion: Jeff Well – Port Angeles, Washington, USA.

2nd: Andre Nathusius – Berliner Bartclub; Berlin, Germany.

3rd: Martin Trendle – Schnauz und Bartclub Rheintal; Trubbach, Switzerland.

Famous Historical Moustaches:
Albert Einstein, Charles De Gaul, Vladimir Lenin, Teddy Roosevelt, Salvador Dali

Previous page: Jeff Well – Port Angeles, Washington, USA
Opposite: Martin Trendle – Schnauz und Bartclub Rheintal; Trubbach, Switzerland

CATEGORY 4
Handlebar MOUSTACHE

⊙ ⊙ ⊙ ⊙

CATEGORY 4

Handlebar Moustache

Small bushy moustache; upward pointing ends; areas past the corners of the mouth will be shaven. Artificial styling aids permitted.

2001 Defending World Champion: Josef Auchter – Schwabisher Bartclub; Germany.

2003 World Champion: Gary Hagen – Handlebar Club/Team USA; Gilroy, California.

2nd: Maury Apfel – Carson City, Nevada, USA.
3rd: Herbert Braunschmid – Belle Moustache; Leinfelden-Echterdingen, Germany.

Moustachioed Entertainers:
Charlie Chaplin, Burt Reynolds, Errol Flynn, Groucho Marx, Clark Gable, Tom Selleck, Dick Dastardly

Opposite:
Gary Hagen – Handlebar Club /Team USA; Gilroy, California

CATEGORY 5
Wild West MOUSTACHE

⊙ ⊙ ⊙ ⊙

CATEGORY 5

Wild West Moustache

Large bushy moustache; whiskers will be brushed from the middle to the side of the upper lip; areas more than 1.5cm (0.6in) past the corners of the mouth will be shaven. Artificial styling aids permitted.

1997, 1999, 2001 Three-time defending World Champion: Guenter Rosin – Schwabisher Bartclub; Schoemberg, Germany.

2003 World Champion: Guenter Rosin – Schwabisher Bartclub; Schoemberg, Germany.

2nd: Josef Ibach – Berliner Bartclub; Berlin, Germany.

3rd: Bruce Roe – Whisker Club/Team USA; Bremerton, Washington, USA.

Opposite and previous spread: Bruce Roe – Whisker Club/Team USA; Bremerton, Washington, USA

CATEGORY 6

Fu manchu

○ ○ ○ ○

CATEGORY 6

Fu manchu

Areas other than the upper lip and those up to 2cm (0.8in) past the corners of the mouth and downward along the side of the chin will be shaven. Ends long and pointed downwards. Artificial styling aids permitted.

2001 Defending World Champion: Juergen Gunther – Kurpfaelzischer Bartclub; Heddesheim, Germany.

2003 World Champion: Ted Sedman – Handlebar Club; London, England.

2nd: Paul Miller – Alta Loma, California, USA.

✂ The oldest competitor in 2003, aged 82, was the Handlebar Club's Alf Jarrald of Manchester, England.

Opposite: Paul Miller – Alta Loma, California, USA. *Previous spread:* Ted Sedman – Handlebar Club; London, England

CATEGORY 7

Imperial MOUSTACHE

CATEGORY 7

Imperial Moustache

Whiskers growing from the cheeks and upper lip; whiskers growing from the cheeks point upward; chin will be shaven. Artificial styling aids allowed.

1999 World Champion: Karl-Heinz Hille – Berliner Bartclub; Berlin, Germany.
2001 Defending World Champion: Juergen Burkhardt – Belle Moustache; Leinfelden-Echterdingen, Germany.

2003 World Champion:
Karl-Heinz Hille – Berliner Bartclub; Berlin, Germany.

2nd: Franz Mitterhauser – Hofener Bartclub; Stockerau, Austria.
3rd: Juergen Burkhardt – Belle Moustache; Leinfelden-Echterdingen, Germany.

Fastest Moustaches: Mark Spitz, Michael Johnson

Previous spread: Karl-Heinz Hille – Berliner Bartclub; Berlin, Germany
Opposite: Franz Mitterhauser – Hofener Bartclub; Stockerau, Austria

CATEGORY 8
Freestyle MOUSTACHE

⊙ ⊙ ⊙ ⊙

CATEGORY 8

Freestyle Moustache

All moustaches not described by any other category. Creativity encouraged. Areas more than 1.5cm (0.6in) past the corners of the mouth will be shaven. Artificial styling aids permitted, encouraged.

1999 World Champion: Frank Werthwein – Germany.
2001 Defending World Champion: Willi Steidle – Germany.

2003 World Champion:
Guenther Krauss – Ostbayrischer Bartclub; Amberg, Germany.

2nd: Lars Olav Braa – Den Norske Mustachclub; Trondheim, Norway.
3rd: Arved Leichsenring – Hofener Bartclub; Hoefen/Enz, Germany.

Opposite: Arved Leichsenring – Hofener Bartclub; Hoefen/Enz, Germany

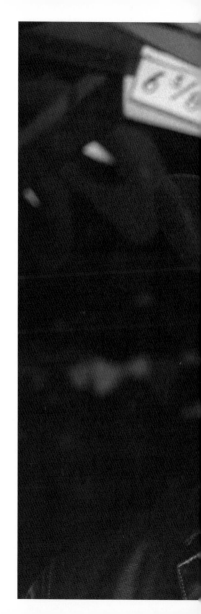

CATEGORY 9

Natural GOATEE

CATEGORY 9

Natural Goatee

Cheeks will be shaven. Moustache optional. No artificial styling aids permitted.

2001 Defending World Champion: Rudolf Wilczek – Schwabisher Bartclub; Schoemberg, Germany.

2003 World Champion: Tie – Gerhard Meuller, Schwabisher Bartclub; Schoemberg, Germany.
Dieter Gugel – Hoefen, Germany.

3rd: Doug Claussen – Whisker Club/ Team USA; Seabeck, Washington, USA.

✃ US ski team member and 2003/04 overall World Cup Downhill Champion Daron Rahlves was a judge at the World Beard and Moustache Championships

Opposite: Gerhard Meuller, Schwabisher Bartclub; Schoemberg, Germany. *Previous spread:* Dieter Gugel – Hoefen, Germany

Musketeer
CATEGORY 10
◉ ◉ ◉ ◉

CATEGORY 10

Musketeer

Small pointed goatee clearly separated from the moustache, which will be especially prominent. Artificial styling aids permitted.

1999 World Champion: Jurgen Draheim – Berliner Bartclub; Berlin, Germany.
2001 Defending World Champion: Reinhard Burcker – Schwabischer Bartclub; Schoemberg, Germany.

2003 World Champion: Gary Johnson – Whisker Club/Team USA; Olalla, Washington, USA.

2nd: Juergen Draheim – Berliner Bartclub; Berlin, Germany.
3rd: Reinhard Burcker – Schwabischer Bartclub; Schoemberg, Germany.

The youngest competitor in 2003 was 17-year-old Cameron Bynum of Reno, Nevada.

Opposite: Gary Johnson – Whisker Club/Team USA; Olalla, Washington, USA
Previous spread: Reinhard Burcker – Schwabischer Bartclub; Schoemberg, Germany

Sideburns
CATEGORY II

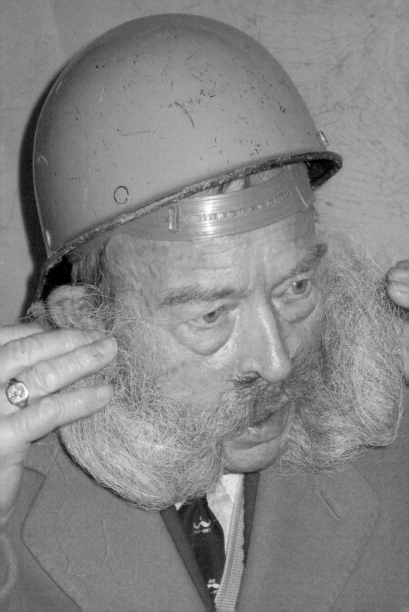

CATEGORY II

Sideburns

May be any length, moustache optional. Chin will be clean shaven. Artificial styling aids permitted.

2003 World Champion: Alf Jarrald – Handlebar Club; London, England.

2nd: Uwe Wankmuller – Germany.
3rd: Bruno Panza – Italy.

Previous spread, left and opposite: Alf Jarrald – Handlebar Club; London, England

Coolest Sideburns: Elvis, Fonzie

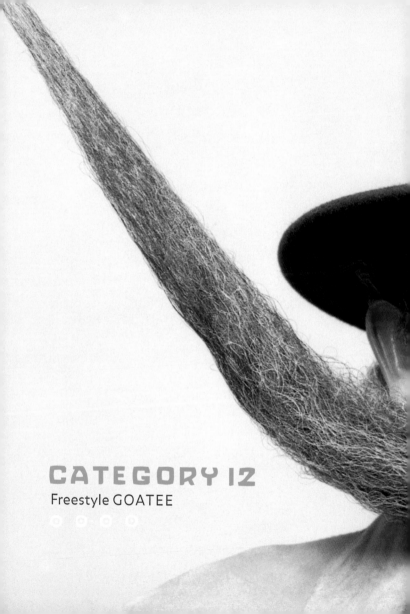

CATEGORY 12

Freestyle GOATEE

CATEGORY 12

Freestyle Goatee

Sideburns will be clean shaven, otherwise, anything goes; creativity encouraged. Artificial styling aids permitted, applauded.

1999 World Champion: Dietmar Stohr – Schwabischer Bartclub; Germany.
2001 Defending World Champion: Willi Chevalier – Hofener Bartclub; Hofen/Enz, Germany.

2003 World Champion: Jurg Biland – Team Switzerland; Gipf-Oberfrick, Switzerland.

2nd: Friedrich Schadel – Kurpfalz Bartclub; Germany.
3rd: Gerhard Knapp – Pforzheim Bartclub; Pforzheim, Germany.

⚡ Bram Rosenfeld of Hong Kong schlepped his moustache 6,954 miles to qualify for the most far-fetched facial hair

Opposite: Jurg Biland – Team Switzerland; Gipf-Oberfrick, Switzerland.
Previous spread: Friedrich Schadel – Kurpfalz Bartclub; Germany

⊙ ⊙ ⊙ ⊙
CATEGORY 13
Full BEARD
Natural

CATEGORY 13

Full Beard Natural

Full beard flowing downward with fully integrated moustache. No artificial styling aids permitted!!

1999 World Champion: Franz Pill – Schwabischer Bartclub; Germany.
2001 Defending World Champion: Paul Boschert – Hofener Bartclub; Germany.

2003 World Champion: Dave Traver – Team USA; Anchorage, Alaska, USA.

2nd: Alois Plettl – Ostbayrischer Bartclub; Passau, Germany.
3rd: Paul Boschert – Hofener Bartclub; Nordrach, Germany.

✄ Prior to the event, the WBMC received written, spoken and broadcast press in 14 nations on 5 continents

Famous Religous Beards: God, Jesus, Moses

Dave Traver – Team USA; Anchorage, Alaska, USA. *Previous spread:* Herbert Dobner – Hoefen-Enz, Germany

CATEGORY 14

Full BEARD Styled Moustache

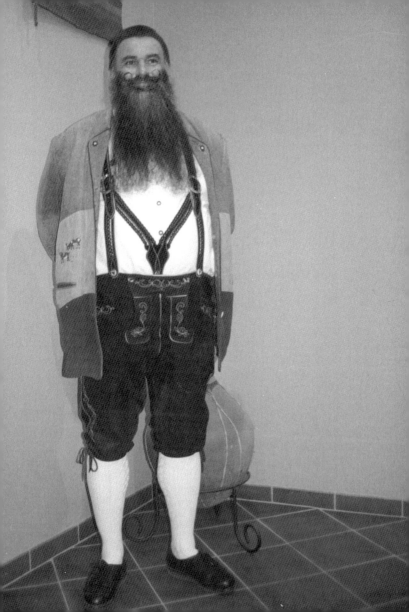

CATEGORY 14

Full Beard Styled Moustache

Beard flows downward without the use of any artificial styling aid; the moustache is styled with artificial styling aids.

2001 Defending World Champion: Hans Horst – Germany.

2003 World Champion:
Karl-Heinz Rein – Hoefen, Germany.

2nd: Bruce Hagen – Paradise, California, USA.
3rd: Wilhelm Preuss – Ostbayrischer Bartclub; Sulzbach-Rosenberg, Germany.

✂ The 2003 WBMC was held on 1 November, Nevada Day. Nevada Day celebrates Nevada's admission as the 36th state in the Union in 1864 by bearded president Abraham Lincoln.

Opposite: Sweet Water John, Virginia City, Nevada *(left)* and Karl-Heinz Rein – Hoefen, Germany. *Previous spread:* Hans Horst, Moos, Germany

CATEGORY 15

Garibaldi

CATEGORY 15

Garibaldi

Wide and full beard with integrated moustache. No artificial styling aids permitted.

2001 Defending World Champion: Franz-Peter Pill – Schoemberg, Germany.

2003 World Champion: Gerhard Schmidbauer – Ostbayrischer Bartclub; Kapfelberg, Germany.

2nd: Franz-Peter Pill – Schoemberg, Germany.

3rd: Fritz Sendlhofer – Ostbayrischer Bartclub; Zell am See, Austria.

⋟ There are over 23 beard clubs in 9 European countries, the Ukraine, and the United States.

Entertaining Beards: Sean Connery, Jerry Garcia, Barry White, Bob Ross, David Bellamy, Billy Connelly

Opposite: Fritz Sendlhofer – Ostbayrischer Bartclub; Zell am See, Austria.
Previous spread: Franco Gherardi

CATEGORY 16
Verdi

CATEGORY 16

Verdi

Bottom round, beard shorn relatively short; cheeks slightly shaven; moustache prominent. No artificial styling aids permitted.

2001 Defending World Champion: Durmus Sensoy – Schwabischer Bartclub; Germany.

2003 World Champion: Marcus Bross – Schoemberg, Germany.

2nd: Willi Segalotto – Schwabischer Bartclub; Geislingen, Germany.
3rd: Peter Diehm – Pforzheim Bartclub; Germany.

✂ Barbate: bearded; having long, stiff hairs

Make Believe Beards: Rip Van Winkle, Santa Claus, Sherlock Holmes

Opposite: Verdi contestants in the parade before the 2002 European Championships in Carvico, Italy
Previous spread: August Schmid, Obermumpf, Switzerland

CATEGORY 17

Full BEARD
Freestyle

◉ ◉ ◉ ◉

CATEGORY 17

Full Beard Freestyle

All beards that do not belong in any other category. Creativity encouraged. Artificial styling aids permitted, often exhausted.

1999 World Champion: Heinz Wirth – Germany.
2001 Defending World Champion: Elmar Weisser – Schwabischer Bartclub; Germany.

2003 World Champion:

Hans Gassner – Ostbayrischer Bartclub; Regenstauf, Germany.

2nd: Elmar Weisser – Schwabischer Bartclub; Brigachtal, Germany.
3rd: Heinz Christofel – Kurpfaelzischer Bartclub; Mannheim, Germany.

Entrepreneurial Beards: Colonel Sanders

Opposite: Hans Gassner – Ostbayrischer Bartclub; Regenstauf, Germany
Previous spread: Heinz Christofel – Kurpfaelzischer Bartclub; Mannheim, Germany

Gary Hagen –
Handlebar Champion

"People hang ornaments on my moustache at Christmas time," says Gary Hagen. Hagen works at a Safeway supermarket in Gilroy, California. His moustache, though technically in conflict with Safeway's strict rules on employee appearance, is a popular attraction in Hagen's hometown. "All times of the year, people are giving me stuff to hang off my moustache."

On the Friday night prior to the WBMC, Hagen was dressed conservatively in an orange sweater and tan chinos. His moustache was more flamboyantly outfitted. It was a patriotic emblem, waxed stiff and sectioned into even areas of dyed red, white and blue. The middle, frosty white section was additionally equipped with a battery powered flashing American Flag pendant.

In the Carson City hotel lobby, a steady stream of passersby had unwavering eyes hard-fixed on Gary's steadily blinking moustache. He didn't seem to notice as he relayed a story from a Valentine's Day past: "...so for half a day I had women's earrings hanging off my moustache and I was thinking 'God, do I look *stupid*.'"

Gary Hagen is a history buff; he is currently a member of both the Horseless Carriage Club of America and the Model-T Club of America. His hobbies engross him. When he donned his elaborate event costume for the WBMC, he first became a leisurely, aristocratic, and dapper 1914 motorist. Secondly, Gary Hagen became the World Handlebar Moustache Champion.

Gary's was the first victory for Team USA. Americans had upsets in many fields and while there were cries of hometown favouritism when more Yankees triumphed in one day than in the WBMC's entire 13 year history, Gary's championship Handlebar didn't raise any eyebrows. His was an obvious winner.

Berlin will host the next championships in 2005. It is unclear how many Americans will travel to defend their titles.

Late in the evening following his triumph, Gary Hagen was back in the hotel lobby. He had yet to change out of his touring clothes; with his black leather driving gloves draped across the concierge desk he gracefully absorbed compliments on his outfit and his win. Then, turning a wistful eye towards the ceiling, he asked no one in particular, "How much *is* the plane fare to Berlin?"

✂ Gary Hagen once tried to style his Handlebar with Elmer's carpentry glue; it was not stiff enough to hold.

✂ After experimenting with candle wax and paraffin, Gary Hagen now incorporates beeswax into his styling mixture.

✂ Gary Hagen once used a curling iron on his moustache and, in a malfunction, burned an inch of hair off one side.

✂ Gary Hagen currently sports the seventh version of his moustache.

✂ Gary Hagen, World Handlebar Champion, once used women's green eye shadow to dye his moustache for Saint Patrick's Day.

Following spread: Rod Littlewood, Alf Jarrald, Ted Sedman *(left to right)* Handlebar Club, England

✂ If you straightened the massive nests of Alf Jarrald's champion Sideburns, they would measure 18 inches on either side

The Handlebar Club
of London

London's Handlebar Club was formed in April 1947 in the dressing room of comedian and RAF WWII pilot Jimmy Edwards at the Windmill Theatre in London. So begins the storied history of Britain's most legendary male hair club.

The object of the club was stated then and remains "to bring together moustache wearers (beards being strictly prohibited) socially for sport and general conviviality".

The club's membership peaked in the 1950s and 60s with about 22 members. Since a curious decline in the disco days of the 1970s, the club maintains an approximate 100 chap membership.

By forming satellite clubs referred to as "nests", the Handlebar Club has spread mustachioed enthusiasm around the UK and Europe.

At the 2003 WBMC, the Handlebar Club was well represented, most notably by club president Ted Sedman's Guinness World Record holding (Britain's longest) moustache that formed his first place Fu manchu.

Still, the real British hero of the day was Alf Jarrald. At 82, Jarrald was by some years the oldest competitor and a determined sport throughout the grueling nine hour contest in Carson City. For his effort, Jarrald and his sideburn nests walked away not only with a first in Sideburns, but also the second place Overall Title.

Jarrald is a slight man and with a small face bracketed by such massive nests of hair, he looks more like a squirrel than any other human on earth. When he hoisted his trophy above his head, the spectators went bananas. In America, Alf Jarrald is loved.

During his years in the RAF during the Second World War, Jarrald had his sideburns "forcibly shorn off a couple of times". After his victories in Carson City, he reaped his hairy benefits. Making the rounds with his trophies, Jarrald was bombarded by youthful women, all wanting a smooch from the elder champion.

The German Imperials

Prior to the opening ceremonies of the WBMC, boisterous bearded Germans were drinking brown beers and laughing hearty laughs. A white-bearded, red-robed and altogether convincing Saint Nick imposter was downing his ale with alarming speed. Outside the Carson City Community Center, they drank in the Nevada sunshine and waited for the opening parade of nations to begin.

Juergen Burkhardt stood quietly, just to the outside of the group of his drunken countrymen. His military dress uniform, complete with silken sash and medals of commendation, was spotlessly clean. He wore wire-rimmed spectacles and a black gilded helmet with a spike pointing flippantly unto the sky. His huge brown Imperial moustache shone in the afternoon light. His moustache was stupendous.

Burkhardt was the Overall Champion and Imperial Champion of the 1997 WBMC in Trondheim, Norway, and the winner of the Imperial category in 2001 in Schoemberg, Germany. In Carson City, Burkhardt was defending a winning legacy.

An Imperial is the flagship of the moustache fleet. It is a lifestyle, this moustache. When not styled, Juergen's hangs nearly to his waistline. It requires great care, waking early in the morning to shape and style. Curlers are used along with sprays, waxes and lacquers to form, in Burkhardt's words, "a harmony of curves". An hour is not an unusually long time to spend molding the proper Imperial.

In Germany, an Imperial recalls images of Kaiser Wilhelm II and evokes memories of an oft-overlooked chapter of German history. For a brief moment at the

opening of the 20th century, a not very hostile Germany was in keeping with its colonizing neighbours – staking out far off lands, building a navy, and sending men with strange facial hair jumping off boats and sticking flags in any good-looking real estate.

The so-called "Sun King" of Germany's Second Reich, Wilhelm was the grandson of Britain's Queen Victoria and, with great admiration for her Empire, triggered Germany's quest for imperial expansion. For Germans, Wilhelm's era would prove a sunnier memory than successive world wars.

When asked about the moustache inspiring Kaiser, Burkhardt began a rambling tale. With an idle camera dangling at his uniformed hip (Burkhardt is also a professional photographer), Juergen told of the Kaiser being the original German photographer – how the King would wait until perfect sunshine before shooting any film. Never pleased in darkness or rain, Kaiser Wilhelm wanted sunshine both for his photos and the German Volk. The Kaiser felt that Germans had staked a "place in the sun" and that this sun-soaked spot would remain German "in order that the sun's rays may fall fruitfully upon our activity".

As the WBMC contestants waited for the parade of nations to begin, the sun was bathing the bearded men in light, but Burkhardt never touched his camera as he spoke at length about Wilhelm II. He squinted at the sky and droned wistfully on towards his culminating point. "When the sun shines," he proclaimed, "We say ... it is ... Kaiser Wetter!" Methodical and rough as it was, pride shone through the cracks of his broken English.

Are all Germans so unabashedly nostalgic for their brief imperial history? Why were only Germans and Austrians competing in the Imperial Moustache category? The British had a fractured empire to be boastful of, yet were clearly not attacking the WBMC with the same fervour as their Germanic counterparts.

When asked why, the British competitors offered little more than a shoulder shrug. "It's a Prussian thing, maybe," thought one Londoner. The British were in it for fun. They had no more explanation for the Prussian seriousness, that drive towards victory absolute, than anyone ever has.

Previous spread: Juergen Burkhardt – Belle Moustache; Leinfelden-Echterdingen, Germany. *Opposite:* Franz Mitterhauser

The Whisker Club – Gary Johnson & Doug Claussen

Gary Johnson of Olalla, Washington has been a member of the only fully functioning beard club in the United States – the Whisker Club of Bremerton, WA – since its inception in 1998. Since then, he has won four Best In Show awards in the Whisker Club's annual competition.

Gary Johnson came to Carson City with long-time friend and fellow Whisker Club member Doug Claussen. For most of the weekend, both men were costumed: Johnson as a gun-toting, Wild West musketeer, clad fully in raw leather and Claussen as a bowler-hatted, bat-wielding Bowery Boy.

Doug's hair, grandiose as his goatee may be, is limited to his face. Save the blond and red and brown whiskers of his goatee, the rest of his head is shaved to a shiny luster. Compared to Gary's imposing frame and booming voice, Doug's role was that of reserved, yet fiercely loyal sidekick. This is not to say he was silent. Doug Claussen has stories of his own that, when proffered from behind the thick curtain of his baleen-like moustache, take a bit of concentration to interpret. The substantially goateed are exempt from lip reading.

Both men have so much hair on their faces, one question instantly comes to mind. What about sex? For a woman, there's just no ignoring the fact that her man has more hair around his mouth than most do on the whole head. Maybe this leads to less face to face lovemaking – the beastlier the man, the more animalistic the fornication.

"They used to say moustache rides cost a nickel – well, they cost a lot more than that nowadays!" Johnson announced while twirling the ends of his foot-long waxed Musketeer. "Oh, women love this stuff, oh yeah, you bet;" he wore the full pointy-whiskered Cheshire-cat grin of a man who could recall some choice memories to back his claims.

Opposite: Doug Claussen. *Following spread:* Gary Johnson

Both married, Gary and Doug originally became friends through their wives, not their whiskers. Their spouses did not accompany them to the WBMC though. "They don't like coming around when we're all acting like a couple idiots."

Both men were excited to be in costume for the championship weekend. Johnson, in particular, seemed to become his costume – the strutting Wild Western outlaw, as ready to shake your hand as put you on the ground with one swing of his massive rawhide wrapped forearms. With tassels flying, you'd never see it coming.

Gary and Doug are at ease in costume and for good reason. Back in Washington state, they involve themselves in "a lot of charity benefits, parades and getting out in the public", Johnson explained. Both men take pride in their faces. Johnson's tri-tipped creation is fashion; it is pure male animal plumage. The two strutted through the Nevada Day Parade and eventually the championships with style. From head to toe, these two delivered what Carson City Mayor Ray Masayko called "the whole package".

Style. It was why Doug Claussen swaggered off stage with a third place Natural Goatee. It gave Gary Johnson and his ever-present grin the Musketeer gold. Johnson wasn't dressed as an authentic musketeer, per se, but whatever the costume was, it was complete. His vision of his own style was full and he was thusly rewarded.

➤ When competing, it takes Gary Johnson 1 hour to dress and prepare his facial hair

Famous Historical Beards: Abraham Lincoln, Rasputin, Genghis Khan, Karl Marx, Black Beard, Charles Darwin, Socrates, George Bernard Shaw, Sigmund Freud

Willi Chevalier and the Great German Schadenfreude

At the WBMC, the Overall prize is awarded to the mustachioed, goateed or bearded man whose facial creation is deemed Best In Show. At the 2001 WBMC held in Hoefen, Germany, the overall title went to Willi Chevalier. Chevalier's freestyle beard was a fabulous creative coup: a beard that seemed to defy physics while attaining true barbate virtuosity.

Tragically, Chevalier and his champion beard suffered a serious injury on 4 October 2003, not a month before he was to defend his title in Carson City. A construction worker by trade, Chevalier had his beard ensnarled in a power drill and ripped from his face. The trauma nearly cost him an eye. The injuries were extensive and disfiguring.

As homage to Chevalier, 2003 WBMC organizer Phil Olsen emblazoned all official championship merchandise with Chevalier's image. His spectacular beard was show-cased on everything from posters to t-shirts.

Olsen was not aware that the Association of German Beard Clubs does not recognize Chevalier's Hoefen Beard Club. In a stunning lack of sympathy, competitors from rival clubs boycotted the images of Chevalier's beard. The tribute, rather than drawing compassion, merely fanned the flames of fierce beard club loyalty. Few Germans bought shirts, but many revelled in that famous German concept: Schadenfreude.

✄ If you are a clean-shaven wanted man, growing a beard or moustache functions as an excellent disguise

Willi Chevalier
Best In Show at
the 2001 WBMC

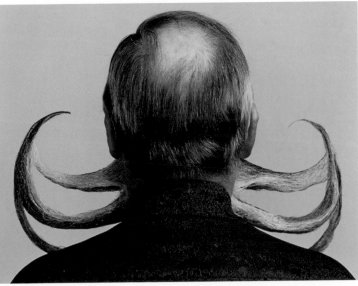

1997
Trondheim, Norway
Jurgen Burkhardt – Belle Moustache;
Leinfelden-Echterdingen, German

1999
Ystad, Sweden
Karl-Heinz Hille – Berliner Bartclub;
Berlin, Germany

OVERALL AWARDS

1997–2003

2001
Schoemberg, Germany
Willi Chevalier – Hofener Bartclub;
Hoefen, Germany

2003
Carson City, USA
Karl-Heinz Hille – Berliner Bartclub;
Berlin, Germany

People's Choice Award:
Heinz Christofel –
Kurpfaelzischer Bartclub;
Mannheim, Germany

Best in Show Award:
1999 World Champion:
Karl-Heinz Hille –
Berliner Bartclub; Berlin, Germany.
2001 World Champion: Willi Chevalier –
Hofener Bartclub; Hoefen, Germany.

2003 World Champion:
Karl-Heinz Hille – Berliner
Bartclub; Berlin, Germany.

2nd: Alf Jarrald –
The Handlebar Club;
Manchester, England.
3rd: Dave Traver – Team
USA; Anchorage, Alaska.

➳ German competitors earned 30 gold medals at
the 2003 WBMC. Team USA was a distant runner-
up with 9 gold medals.

Above: People's Choice Award: Heinz Christofel –
Kurpfaelzischer Bartclub; Mannheim, Germany

2003 World Champion: Karl-Heinz Hille –
Berliner Bartclub; Berlin, Germany

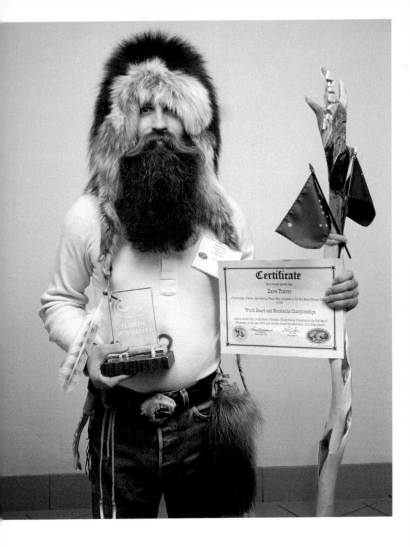

2003 3rd place overall: Dave Traver –
Team USA; Anchorage, Alaska

THE CHAMPION

Style. In the end, it was the deciding factor. It awarded men who had defined their presence and the actions within that presence. It gave Heinz Christofel of Mannheim, Germany, the People's Choice Award for a weekend of unselfconscious parading. "I am Captain Hook," he said with piratical mischief as he accepted his award.

Style brought the World Beard and Moustache Championships into being. The pursuit of Style united the men, driving them into competition.

It moved the crowd when Karl-Heinz Hille emerged from the rear of the stage to claim his Overall Best in Show. In Carson City, the capital town of the Silver State, an untarnished gentleman, the distinguished Imperial champion, triumphs.

Hille: a vision of silver, a tableau of affectation and mustachioed flair so perfect no one could compete. His snow white Imperial, extending upwards from his cheeks in a luminescent half moon, Hille was always going to win. No one questioned it. His civilian regality outranked the Prussian military types surrounding him. His shimmering three-piece suit, accented by his silver top hat, his silver-rimmed spectacles, his silver ascot, his shimmering silver cane, and his spotless white gloves all carried with perfect posture, perfectly timed cane taps and perfect astonishment, when he eventually won it all.

Opposite: Gerhard Schmidbauer, Heinz Christofel *(in red)* and Karl-Heinz Hille

✂ Bruce Hagen *(below),* Paradise, California, USA, runner-up for Full Beard Styled Moustache, once turned down a job at a cemetery that would have required him to shave.

✂ Gary James Chilton *(above)* was the Iowa State Fair Beard Champion for six years running before attending the 2003 WBMC. His 26-year-old beard measures 41.5 inches.

✂ Many felt that Chilton's exclusion from the medal podium was a great injustice at the 2003 WBMC.

✂ Phil Olsen *(Opposite)*, the 2003 WBMC organizer, speaks German and Norwegian and is conversational in Swedish and Italian. His language skills made him the perfect barbate diplomat.

Yes,
I'm Santa

✂ There are over 23 beard clubs in 9 European countries, the Ukraine, and the United States. With 9, Germany sports nearly half of all the world's beard clubs

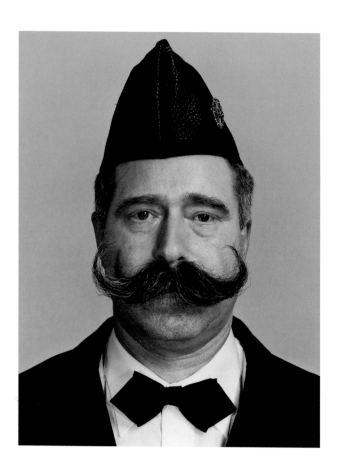

A snood is a protective moustache sock worn during periods of rest or prolonged travel.

A moustache cup is equipped with a shelf on which a moustache rests, thereby staying dry and untouched by a beverage, hot or cold.

A moustache spoon has a small extending arm to pour liquid into a mustachioed man's mouth rather than his moustache.

Afterword
by Phil Olsen, 2003 WBMC event organiser

IN OCTOBER 2002, the Association of German Beard Clubs extended me the honor of organizing a World Beard and Moustache Championship - the first of its kind in America - to be hosted the following year in Nevada.

Soon thereafter, I formed a website and corporation to organize the event; the response was huge. The internet proved to be the ultimate marketing tool and was soon receiving thousands of visits per day. By 1 November, 2003, the day of the WBMC, 123 contestants from nine countries had arrived in Carson City, Nevada for the big event.

Prior to 2003, the WBMC had been hosted by Norway, Sweden and Germany. The next Championships will be held on 1 October, 2005 in Berlin, Germany. The event will coincide with the annual celebration commemorating the fall of the Berlin Wall, a national German holiday. It promises to be another hugely exciting competition.

See you in Berlin!

WORLD BEARD AND MOUSTACHE CHAMPIONSHIPS 1 October 2005
Tegelerseeterrassen, Tegel Lake, Berlin, Germany
REGISTRATION FORM Entry Fee €25

Name: . . . . Age: . . . .

Address: . . . .

. . . . Email: . . . .

Phone: . . . . Fax: . . . .

Name of Beard Club if applicable: . . . .

Category: Prior to the competition, the judges will determine whether each competitor qualifies for the category he has chosen and will be placed into the appropriate category in accordance with the AGBC rules.

Please circle category for entry:
Moustaches: [1. Natural] [2. English] [3. Dali] [4. Handlebar]
[5. Wild West] [6. Fu manchu] [7. Imperial] [8. Freestyle]
Goatees: [9. Natural Goatee] [10. Musketeer] [11. Freestyle Goatee]
Beards: [12. Full Beard Natural] [13. Full Beard Styled Moustache]
[14. Garibaldi] [15. Verdi] [16. Full Beard Freestyle]

I hereby consent to being photographed as a participant in this event.
I further consent to my image appearing on television.

Signature . . . .

Please bring a copy of the completed form with you to the competition in Berlin. Participants will be automatically registered upon receipt of the form but competitors will also be able to register on the day of the competition. For more information check out:
www.worldmoustachechampion.com or www.worldbeardchampionships.com

| Mail completed form to: | Berlin Bartclub c/o Lutz Giese Krowelstrasse 10 D-13581 Berlin Germany | Tel: 0049 30 8731789 Email: lugi4712@freenet.de lgiese@1-berliner-bart-club.de |

The 2007 World Beard and Moustache Championships will take place in England to celebrate the 60th anniversary of the founding of the oldest moustache club in the world – The Handlebar Club. For more information contact: The Handlebar Club, c/o Ted Sedman, 7 Mytchett Heath, Mytchett, Camberley, Surrey GU16 6DP, United Kingdom
ted@sedman.org Tel.: (+44) 1252 545432